A
an   ia

Heinemann
LIBRARY

www.heinemann.co.uk/library

Visit our website to find out more information about Heinemann Library books.

To order:
☎ Phone 44 (0) 1865 888066
Send a fax to 44 (0) 1865 314091
Visit the Heinemann Bookshop at www.heinemann.co.uk/library to browse our catalogue and order online.

First published in Great Britain by Heinemann Library, Halley Court, Jordan Hill, Oxford OX2 8EJ, part of Harcourt Education. Heinemann is a registered trademark of Harcourt Education Ltd.

Editorial: Kathy Peltan, Clare Lewis, and Katie Shepherd
Design: Joanna Hinton-Malivoire and Q2A Creative
Picture research: Erica Newbery
Production: Helen McCreath

Origination: Modern Age Repro House Ltd.
Printed and bound in China by South China Printing Co. Ltd.

13-digit ISBN 978-0-431-15808-2 (hardback)
10 09 08 07 06
10 9 8 7 6 5 4 3 2 1

13-digit ISBN 978-0-431-09898-2 (paperback)
11 10 09 08 07
10 9 8 7 6 5 4 3 2 1

British Library Cataloguing in Publication Data
Fox, Mary Virginia
Australia and Oceania. – 2nd ed. – (Continents)
919.4
A full catalogue record for this book is available from the British Library.

Acknowledgements
The publishers would like to thank the following for permission to reproduce photographs: Animals Animals: Hans & Judy Beste p. **15**; Bruce Coleman Inc.: Norman Owen Tomalin, p. **14**, **23**, Hans Reinhard p. **16**, Eric Crichton p. **21**, Bob Burch p. **27**; Corbis: Theo Allofs p. **11**, Patrick Ward p. **25**; Earth Scenes: Dani/Jeske pp. **5**, **17**, Michael Fogden, p. **6**; Getty Images: Photographer's Choice/ Ross Woodhall p. **8**; Peter Arnold: J.P. Perrero p. **12**, John Cancalosi p. **19**; Photo Researchers: Georg Gerster p. **22**; A. Flowers & L. Newman, p. **29**; Tony Stone: Robin Smith p. **24**, Doug Armand p. **28**.

Cover photograph of Australia, reproduced with permission of Science Photo Library/ Worldsat International and J. Knighton.

The publishers would like to thank Kathy Peltan, Keith Lye, and Nancy Harris for their assistance in the preparation of this book.

Every effort has been made to contact copyright holders of any material reproduced in this book. Any omissions will be rectified in subsequent printings if notice is given to the publishers.

Some words are shown in bold, **like this**. You can find out what they mean by looking in the glossary.

Contents

Where are Australia and Oceania?

A continent is a very large area of land. There are seven continents in the world. Australia is the smallest continent. Australia is part of a huge **region** called Oceania. It includes New Zealand, Papua New Guinea, and many islands in the Pacific Ocean.

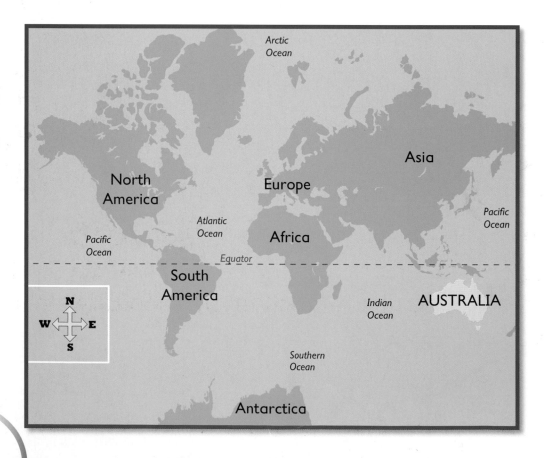

▲ *Australia is a huge island surrounded by sea*

Most of Oceania is below the **Equator**. The Equator is an imaginary line around the centre of the Earth. Australia is much larger than any other land area in Oceania.

Weather

In Australia and New Zealand, winter lasts from June to September. This is summer time in Europe. The weather in most of Australia is very hot and dry. There is a short rainy season. New Zealand is much cooler and wetter.

The dry, bare country away from the Australian coast is called the **outback**.

▲ *The dry land of the Australian outback*

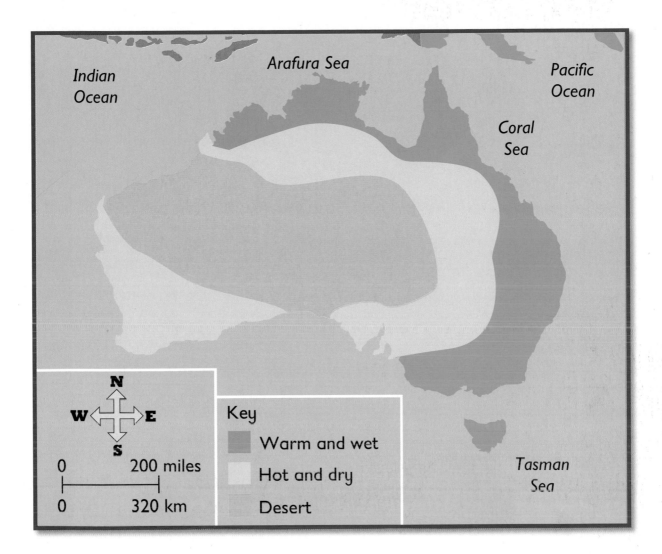

Indian
Ocean

Arafura Sea

Pacific
Ocean

Coral
Sea

N
W **E**
S

0   200 miles

0   320 km

Key

     Warm and wet

     Hot and dry

     Desert

Tasman
Sea

Oceania includes three groups of islands.
They are called Melanesia, Polynesia, and
Micronesia. Northern Australia and many of the
islands of Oceania are close to the **Equator**.
Near the Equator, the weather is hot and wet.

Mountains

▲ *Skiing in New Zealand*

New Zealand has many steep, snow-covered **peaks**. People go skiing and snowboarding there. Australia has only a few high mountains. Its highest mountain is Mount Kosciuszko.

Australia has mountains called the Great Dividing Range. On one side of the mountains it is hot and dry. On the other side it is warm and wet. Most Australians live in cities on the coasts. Few people live in the **deserts** of central Australia.

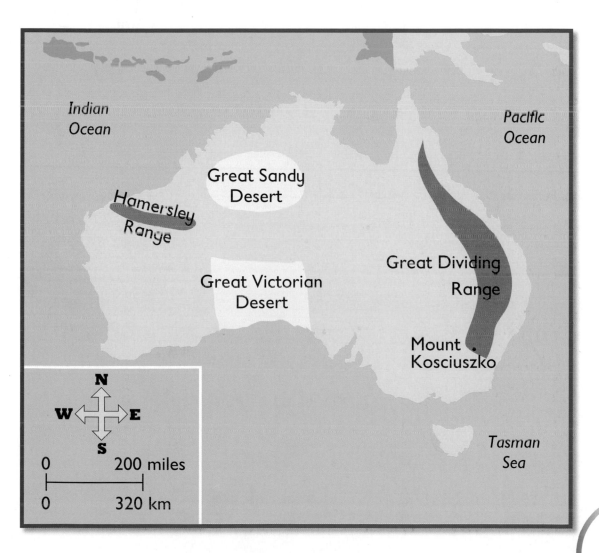

Rivers

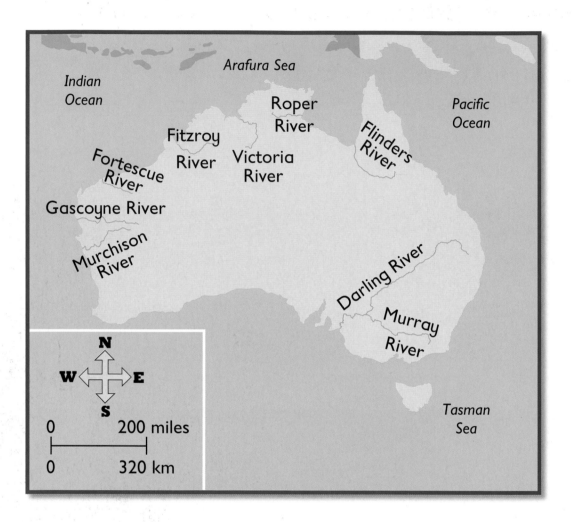

Australia's main rivers are around the edge of the country. The Murray and Darling Rivers join to make the Murray-Darling River. Some of Australia's best farming land is in the Murray Valley.

Some of Australia's rivers dry up completely during the hot summer months. But in the **tropical** islands of Oceania there is heavy rainfall. Rivers there often flood the villages and farmland.

▲ *Dry river in Australia*

Lakes

Lake Eyre is the largest lake in Australia. This **saltwater** lake is almost empty for most of the year. Many Australian lakes dry up for part of the year. This is because there is very little rain.

Lake Eyre has only filled up completely three times in the last 100 years.

▲ *Lake Eyre, South Australia*

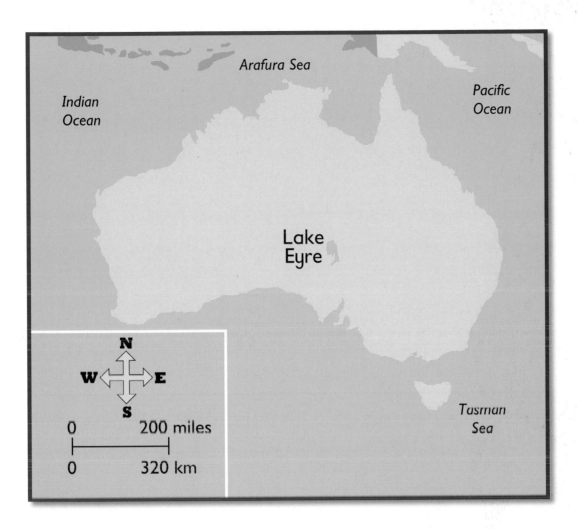

Lake Eyre is the lowest part of Australia. Many tourists visit it. Some of them camp in a large park that surrounds the lake. When the lake is dry, the bottom of it is covered with salt and clay.

Animals

The emu is a big bird. It can run very fast. It cannot fly.

▲ *Galloping emu*

Some very unusual animals live in Oceania. In Papua New Guinea, there are beautiful birds of paradise. They hang upside-down from trees to show off their blue feathers and long tails.

Kangaroos and koalas are only found in Australia. The mothers have **pouches** for carrying their babies. A baby kangaroo is called a joey. The duck-billed platypus has **webbed** feet and a flat beak, like a duck.

▼ *Kangaroo and baby, or joey*

Baby kangaroos are tiny when they are born. They crawl up into their mother's pouch. They stay there for about six months.

Plants

Eucalyptus, or gum trees, grow in many parts of Australia. In the **tropical** islands of Oceania, farmers grow **sugar cane**, bananas, and pineapples. Kiwi fruit, apples, and apricots grow well in New Zealand's cooler weather.

There are more than 500 kinds of gum tree.

▲ *Eucalyptus trees*

▲ *Kangaroo paw*

Wild flowers, such as the prickly kangaroo paw, grow in western Australia. They grow during the rainy season. The seeds of one type of **desert** plant lie in the hot desert for many years, waiting for rain.

People

Around 40,000 years ago people from Southeast Asia began to arrive in northern Australia. The first people to live in Australia were called **Aboriginal people**. They lived in Australia for thousands of years.

▼ *Aboriginal children*

There were once about 250 Australian languages. But only a few are used today.

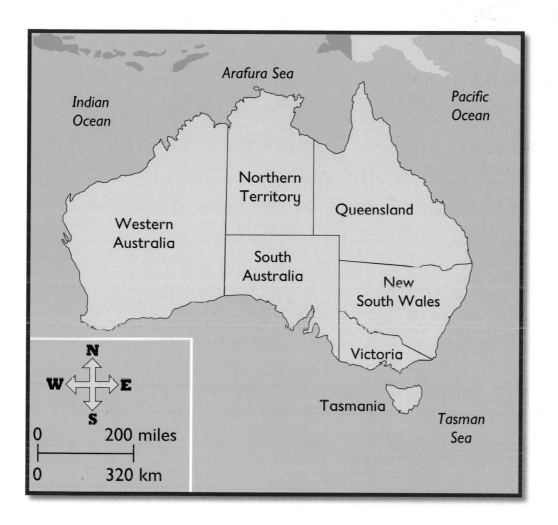

The British explorer Captain Cook sailed to Australia over 200 years ago. Then many people from Europe came to live there. They divided the land into six areas. Many people who lived there began to speak English.

Cities

This map shows some of the most important cities in Australia. The **capital city** of Australia is Canberra. Darwin is a busy port and a centre for **mining**. The Gold Coast has beautiful beaches and many large hotels.

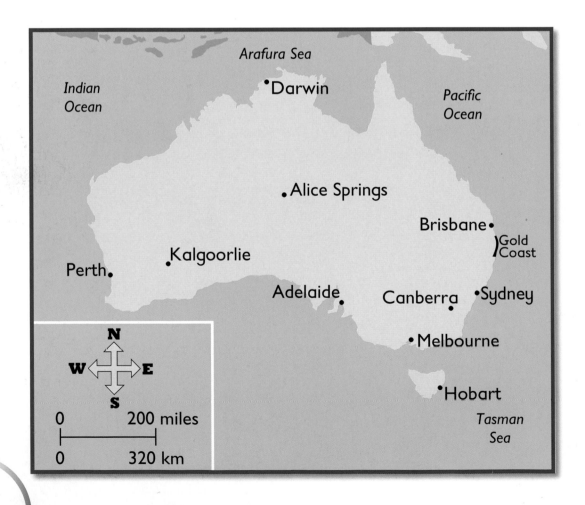

These electric trams take people around the city centre.

▲ *Trams in Melbourne, Victoria*

Melbourne is the second largest city in Australia. It was built with money from gold mining. Now Melbourne is an important centre for art, theatre, and music. There are three universities, as well as many offices and factories.

Large yachts take part in sailing races in the sea around Perth.

▲ *Perth, Western Australia*

Perth is the largest city on Australia's west coast. The largest city in New Zealand is Auckland. Auckland is called the "city of sails" because it is a popular place to go **yachting**.

Most Australians live in the cities along the coasts. Some people live close to the city centre. But many people's homes are in the **suburbs** surrounding the cities.

There is plenty of space in Australia, so the houses usually have large gardens.

▲ *An Australian home in the suburbs*

In the country

Away from the cities, the bare land of the Australian **outback** stretches for thousands of kilometres. Large areas of this land are used for farming. Towns are usually very far apart.

Cattle and sheep farmers live on huge **ranches**, called stations.

▲ *Using a radio to learn lessons*

Most children in the outback live far away from the nearest school. They receive their lessons from the radio or a computer. If people become ill in the outback, the "flying doctor" travels to see them in a small plane.

Famous places

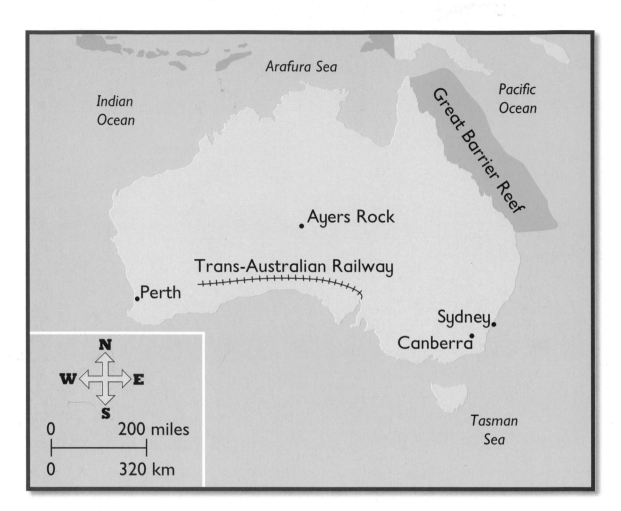

The Trans-Australian Railway runs through the **outback**. Before it was built, people had to walk across the **desert** or ride on camels. Today, many people also choose to travel by aeroplane to get from one city to another.

The Sydney Opera House sits on the shores of Sydney Harbour. Sydney is the oldest and largest city in Australia. The Olympic Games were held there in the year 2000.

The roof of the Sydney Opera House looks like the sails of **yachts**.

▲ *Sydney Opera House*

Uluru is a mountain of red rock in central Australia. It is also called Ayers Rock. Uluru is a sacred place for the **Aboriginal people**. It has many rock paintings on its surface. At sunset, it looks purple.

Uluru is the Aboriginal name for this rock. It means "many heads".

▲ *Uluru, or Ayers Rock*

The Great Barrier Reef is the world's largest coral reef.

▲ *Great Barrier Reef*

The Great Barrier **Reef** runs along the northeast coast of Australia. Coral is made from the skeletons of millions of tiny sea creatures. It grows in many shapes and colours. Thousands of different types of fish swim among the coral.

Fast facts

Some of the highest mountains in Oceania

Name	Height in metres	Height in feet	Area in Oceania
Mt Wilhelm	4,510	14,796	Papua New Guinea
Giluwe	4,368	14,330	Papua New Guinea
Mount Cook	3,764	12,349	New Zealand
Mawson Peak	2,745	9,006	Heard Island
Mt Makarakomburu	2,447	8,028	Solomon Islands

Populations of the biggest and smallest islands in Oceania

Biggest islands	Population	Smallest islands	Population
Australia	20,090,437	Pitcairn Islands	45
Papua New Guinea	5,545,268	Christmas Island	361
New Zealand	4,035,461	Nauru	13,048
Fiji	893,354	Cook Islands	21,388
Solomon Islands	538,032	Marshall Islands	59,071

Australia record-breakers

Towns in Australia can be 150 kilometres (93 miles) apart.

The Great Barrier Reef is the world's largest coral **reef**. It stretches for 2,000 kilometres (1243 miles).

There are over 25,000 islands in Oceania, but only a few thousand have people living on them.

Australia produces a quarter of the world's wool. There are about eight times as many sheep as people in Australia!

Glossary

Aboriginal people first people to live in Australia

capital city city where government leaders work

desert hot, dry area with very little rain

Equator imaginary circle around the exact middle of the Earth

mining digging up things from under the Earth's surface

outback land in Australia away from the cities

peak highest part of a mountain

pouch part on the front of a kangaroo where a baby is kept

ranch very large farm where animals are kept

reef line of underwater rocks or coral close to the surface of the sea

region large area

saltwater water that is salty, like the sea

suburb area of houses at the edge of a big city

sugar cane plant used to make sugar

tropical hot, wet places near the Equator

webbed feet where the toes are joined together, like a duck's feet

yacht sailing boat

More books to read

My World of Geography: Deserts, Angela Royston
   (Heinemann Library, 2004)

Watching Kangaroos in Australia, Louise and Richard Spilsbury
   (Heinemann Library, 2006)

We're from Australia, Vic Parker (Heinemann Library, 2005)

Index